PROFESSIONAL RESOURCES

W9-DHX-257

The Four-Blocks™
Literacy Model

Making Words: Lessons for Home or School Grade 4

by

Patricia M. Cunningham

and

Dorothy P. Hall

Editors

Joey Bland
Tracy Soles

Cover Design

Julie Webb

ISBN 0-88724-663-X

Table of Contents

Introduction

For most teachers, deciding what to give children for homework is a constant concern, similar in many ways to the daily task of deciding what to cook for dinner! When deciding what to cook for dinner, we have to choose foods that will not only fill everyone up, but also have nutritional value. In deciding what homework to give students, we have to make sure that the homework does not just fill time, but also provides practice with important skills. Planning dinner for several people is complicated by the facts that people don't all like the same foods, and different people have different nutritional needs. Planning homework assignments is complicated by the different ability levels of the children—what some children need to practice, others have already mastered, and still others are not ready for.

Making Words is used in many classrooms, and most children view it as a "game-like, puzzle-solving" activity. They enjoy manipulating the letters and are intrigued with the idea that changing just one letter in the word or changing the order of the letters can create a totally different word. They like trying to figure out the secret word and sorting the words they made by spelling patterns. Most children also view figuring out the transfer words based on the sorted rhyming words as a "puzzle to be solved." Teachers like doing Making Words with their students because the students are actually engaged in a "hands-on, minds-on" activity through which they can discover how the English spelling system works and how letters are combined to decode and spell words. Teachers also appreciate the fact that Making Words is a multilevel activity—there is something in each lesson for every level of learner.

Having watched the success of Making Words activities with thousands of teachers and children, and being aware of how difficult it is to come up with good, meaningful, multilevel homework assignments, we began talking about how great it would be to come up with a Making Words lesson format which students could do on their own. As we began, we had some questions. How could we let the students know which words to make? How would the sort and transfer steps work?

The format we developed gives sentence clues, blanks to indicate the number of letters needed, and some basic instructions (add 1 letter, move the letters, etc.). The rhymes and related words are cued by having some letters listed on the sheet, and blanks for each missing letter. The transfer rhyming words have sentences and beginning letter cues. Begin by doing the five warm-up lessons with the class. We have found that some children need to do these warm-up lessons so that they understand the three tasks involved: making words, sorting for patterns and related words, and transferring the patterns to some new/unknown words in sentences. We want all children to be successful when they are asked to do these lessons alone at home.

The Student Lesson Sheet Format

Each lesson sheet has the letters needed across the top. The first thing children should do is to turn the paper over and write the capital letters on the back. This will give students the capital letters they will need if they are making a name. (If the lesson sheet is assigned as homework, it is a good idea to have the students turn their sheets over and write these capital letters before they leave your classroom.) When children begin their assignment, they will <u>cut the letters apart</u> and use these to make the words.

e	e	o	h	m	p	s	r	t	t

Make Words

1. I had to study for my spelling __ __ __.
2. (Change 1 letter.) My little brother ate all the __ __ __ __ of the cookies.
3. (Change 1 letter.) Sometimes my little brother is a real __ __ __ __.
4. (Move the letters.) The baby took his first __ __ __ __ when he was 10 months old.
5. (Add 1 letter.) It was hard work pedaling up the __ __ __ __ __ hill.
6. (Change 1 letter.) We get wool from __ __ __ __ __.
7. The opposite of tall is __ __ __ __ __.
8. (Change 1 letter.) Soccer is a very popular __ __ __ __ __.
9. The children went to the grocery store with their __ __ __ __ __.
10. (Add 4 letters.) The children live with their father and his wife, who is their __ __ __ __ __ __ __.

I wrote a rep_____ on whales for my science class.
The police told the robber that he was under arr_____.

Lesson 11

23

Related Words

m __ __ __
__ __ __ __ m __ __ __

Rhymes

t __ __ __
__ __ __ __
__ __ __ __
s __ __ __ __   s __ __ __ __
__ __ __ __ __   __ __ __ __ __

Name_____

© Carson-Dellosa CD-2611

A sentence is given for each word so that students can use context clues to determine what the word is. For some words, a few letters are also provided. The small lines indicate the number of letters needed to spell each word. Children should make the words with their cut-apart letters and then write the letters on the appropriate lines.

Once all the words have been made, the task is to sort them into rhymes and related words. The area on the right side of the sheet has blanks (and some letters) to indicate the rhyming patterns for which the children will be sorting. In most lessons, there are also some related words—words that share a meaningful part, such as light, lighting, lightning; prison, prisoners; etc. A related word can also be part of a compound word such as some, thing, something; rail, road, railroads; etc.

At the bottom of each sheet, there are sentences with a missing word in each. The missing word is the transfer word, and it uses one of the rhyming patterns from the right side of the sheet. (For some words, the last syllable rhymes with one of the rhyming patterns.) The beginning letters are provided, and the children must choose the correct rhyming pattern to make a word which begins with those letters and makes sense in the sentence.

Teaching Children How to Complete Their Making Words Lesson Sheet

The most effective way to teach children how to complete these lessons on their own is to do several examples with them. We have included five warm-up lessons for you to do with your students. Work through the warm-up lessons with the students, sentence by sentence, completing and checking each word as they do it.

Explain some of the "ground rules" as you do this:

1. The **number of blank lines equals the number of letters needed**.

2. When the instructions say "**add letters**," the letters can be inserted anywhere, but the other letters do not move except to make space for the needed letters. For example, in Warm-Up Lesson One, students add 1 letter to **it** to spell **lit**, 1 letter to **tin** to spell **thin**, 1 letter to **thin** to spell **think**, 3 letters to **light** to spell **lighting**, and 1 letter to **lighting** to get the secret word, **lightning**. If your students understand from the very beginning that they don't ever move the other letters around when following the "add letters" direction, but simply move them to make space, they will be more successful with the lessons.

3. When the instructions say "**change 1 letter**," **only 1 letter should be changed** and the **other letters don't move**. (For example, in Warm-Up Lesson One, students change 1 letter to go from **lit** to **hit**, and change 1 letter again to go from **night** to **light**.) These hints are included so that most of your students will be successful with every word. If students understand these instructions from the very beginning, they will experience more immediate success and be more apt to view the Making Words lesson as a "puzzle to be solved" and a fun activity.

4. When the instructions say "**move the letters**," it means **the word can be made with exactly the same letters as the previous word if the letters are moved to different positions**. For example, in Warm-Up Lesson One, after spelling **thing**, students move the letters to spell **night**. When following the "move the letters" instruction, no letters are added and all the letters from the previous word must be used to spell the new word.

5. Rhyming words with the same spelling patterns should be written in the rhyming word portion of the lesson sheet. The first letter of one of the rhymes and the number of letters in the word will help students find the rhymes.

6. Related words share a word part and some meaning. Related words often include root words with added prefixes and suffixes. Compound words are also related words. One letter shared by all the related words is listed, as well as blanks to indicate how many letters are needed. This should ensure success in sorting the related words.

7. The sentences at the bottom of the sheet can be completed by using the spelling patterns in the rhyming words.

8. Sometimes, it is helpful to work backwards. For example, in Warm-Up Lesson One, imagine that a student just couldn't think of a word for #4 (Some cans are made of ___ ___ ___.), but he could figure out that **thin** is the answer for #5 (The opposite of thick is ___ ___ ___ ___.) Since the instructions for #5 said to add 1 letter from the #4 word, the student can work backwards, take away 1 letter to get the word for #4, and probably figure out that the word is **tin**. Most of your students will figure this out eventually, but if you let them in on the "trick," they will experience more immediate success and participate more willingly.

We have found that once most fourth-graders have done the five warm-up lessons with you, they are ready to tackle the rest of the lessons independently.

Some teachers like the children to have a set of written directions for completing their Making Words homework sheets. The reproducible sheet of directions on page 7 gives directions and reminds children of the helpful tips you have taught them.

Checking the Making Words Lesson Sheet

Children should check their own Making Words Lesson sheets, and the lessons should be completely correct almost all of the time. The easiest and fastest way to check the lesson is to make a transparency of it. Put the transparency on an overhead projector, and let the children tell you what they wrote on their papers as you write the answers on the transparency. Be sure to "brag" on students' success by telling them what good spellers and word decoders they are becoming!

You're the Teacher!

In creating these lessons, we have tried to choose words and provide enough support so that all your students can be successful in doing the activity. We also tried to avoid any words that your students might not have in their listening vocabularies. We argued (good-naturedly) about whether children needed to have one of the letters in a word already filled in to ensure their success. When we completed the lessons, we tried them out with some fourth-graders and made some adjustments. We are working at a disadvantage, however, because we don't know your children. Depending on where you teach and the language level of your children, these lessons may be too hard or too easy. (If they seem too easy, you may want to look at other Making Words lessons which use more sophisticated words, sorts, and transfers based on chunks—including root words, suffixes, and prefixes.) If some of the lessons use words your children do not have in their listening vocabularies or do not provide enough support, you can modify the lesson sheets before giving them to students. Add a few letters to a troublesome word if you think students won't figure it out otherwise. We decided not to provide any letters for the secret words because most children love figuring them out. If most of your children won't be able to get the secret word, then add a few letters before you duplicate the sheet to ensure their success.

As you look at a lesson, if you decide we have provided too many letters and your students will be bored, you can use white correction fluid to obliterate those unneeded letters. (For members of the "computer-only" generation, correction fluid is like thick, white nail polish, and in the good old days, we painted it on typos and then typed over them!)

We have done our best to use our knowledge of and fascination with words to create lessons that would not only move your students forward in their word knowledge, but that your children would also see as a "puzzle they could solve." We ask that you use your knowledge of your students and adjust the lessons as needed, so that they can all experience success as word detectives.

Making Words Lesson Sheet Directions and Tips for Successful Word Detectives

1. Cut the letters apart. Make sure you don't get letters turned around. (The line at the bottom of each letter is your clue.)

2. Move the letters to make words and write the words made in the sentences. (Your clues are what makes sense in the sentence and the number of letters.)

3. Use the instructions (in parentheses) to check yourself. Remember:

   When you **add letters**, don't move the other letters except to make space.

   When you **change one letter**, the other letters don't move.

   When you **move the letters**, the new word will have exactly the same letters as the word you just made, but the letters will be moved to a different place.

4. The last word is the **secret word**, and it uses **all** the letters.

5. Sort for **rhyming words** and write them in the Rhymes section.

6. Sort for the **related words** and write them in the Related Words section. (Some lessons don't have any related words, so there won't be a section for them.)

7. Use the **spelling patterns (vowel to the end) in your rhyming words** to spell rhyming words that make sense in the sentences at the bottom of the lesson page.

8. Sometimes detectives have to **work backwards**! Get all the words you can and then see how these words provide clues for the ones you couldn't get at first.

9. Become a word detective as you do your Making Words lesson sheet. Use all the clues and your clever thinking to solve these puzzles. Enjoy!

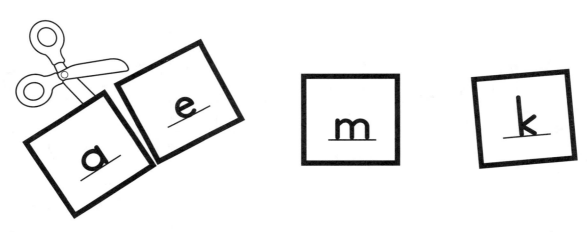

i	i	g	g	h	l	n	n	t

Make Words

1. What time is _____?
2. (Add 1 letter.) We _____ the candles.
3. (Change 1 letter.) The batter got a _____ in the ninth inning.
4. Some cans are made of _____.
5. (Add 1 letter.) The opposite of thick is _____.
6. (Add 1 letter.) My grandpa has everything and I can't think of a _____ to get him for his birthday.
7. (Move the letters.) It gets dark at _____.
8. (Change 1 letter.) Please turn the _____ on.
9. (Add 3 letters.) We are _____ all _____.
10. (Add 1 letter.) We had a bad thunderstorm and the barn was struck by _____ _____.

Related Words

i	—	—	—	
i	—	—	—	—
—	—	—	—	—

Rhymes

i	—	l	—	
—	—	—	—	—
—	—	—	t	—
—	—	—		—

The man got mad and qu_____ his job.

It is against the rules to f_____ on the playground.

Name _____

e	i	o	g	h	m	n	s	t

Make Words

1. Could I please have s _____ more ice cream?

2. We _____ lots of songs in music class.

3. The opposite of thick is _____.

4. (Move the letters.) Can you give me a h _____ about what I am getting for my birthday?

5. (Change the first letter.) I like chocolate _____ ice cream.

6. I want to go to the mall, but I m _____ not be able to.

7. _____ is one of the five senses.

8. (Change 1 letter.) I walk the dog every _____ after dinner.

9. (Move the letters.) Do you know what this _____ is?

10. (Add 4 letters.) I hope my mom is cooking _____ good for dinner.

Related Words

s _____

t _____

s _____ t

Rhymes

_____ m

_____

n _____

_____ s

_____

_____

I knew someone had been there when I saw the footpr _____ in the snow.

When it is dark and I walk the dog, I always take a flashl _____ .

Warm-Up Lesson 2

Name _____

9

e	i	u	u	b	s	s	t	t	t

Make Words

1. Our teacher gives _____ _____ a break in the afternoon.
2. (Add 1 letter.) We ride to school on the _____.
3. (Move the letters.) A _____ _____ can be a sandwich or a boat that goes underwater.
4. (Change 1 letter.) I take a bath in the _____.
5. (Add 1 letter.) We have two _____ _____, one in each bathroom.
6. (Move the letters.) It really hurts when you _____ _____ your toe.
7. I got an A on my spelling _____ _____.
8. (Change 1 letter.) I always try to do my _____ _____ work.
9. Some toothpaste comes in a _____ _____.
10. When our teacher is sick, we have a _____ _____ _____.

Rhymes

u _____

b _____ _____

s _____ _____

_____ _____

_____ _____

_____ _____

My friends and I belong to a cl_____.
California is on the W_____ Coast.

Warm-Up Lesson 3

Name _____

e	i	o	n	p	r	r	s	s

Make Words

1. Our teacher has a pretty ___ ___ on her jacket today.

2. (Add 1 letter.) If you ___ ___ around too much, you will get dizzy.

3. The pitcher had to leave the game because he had a ___ ___ arm.

4. (Move the letters.) We have a red ___ ___ ___ bush in our yard.

5. (Change 1 letter.) Pinocchio had a very long ___ ___ ___ .

6. A p ___ ___ ___ tree has needles and stays green all year.

7. (Add 1 letter.) Your backbone is also called your ___ ___ ___ .

8. I saw the fire truck and heard its loud ___ ___ ___ .

9. The robbers were caught and sent to ___ ___ ___ .

10. (Add 3 letters.) Two ___ ___ ___ escaped from jail.

Related Words

p ___ ___

p ___ ___ ___

Rhymes

p ___ ___ ___   r ___ ___

___ ___ ___

p ___ ___ ___

___ ___ ___

After three days of rain, we were delighted to see the sunsh___ .
Would you please cl___ the door?

Warm-Up Lesson 4

Name ___

a	e	i	d	h	h	r	s	s	w

Make Words

1. I didn't want my little brother to find my new book so I h _____ it.

2. (Add 1 letter.) Sometimes, I _____ _____ things and forget where I put them.

3. (Change 1 letter.) I always walk on the right _____ _____ _____ of the road.

4. (Change 1 letter.) The opposite of narrow is _____ _____ _____.

5. (Change 1 letter.) The opposite of foolish is _____ _____ _____.

6. I put the cat's food in his d _____ _____.

7. I always _____ _____ _____ my hands before I eat.

8. (Change 1 letter.) On my birthday, I make a _____ _____ _____ and then blow out the candles.

9. (Add 2 letters.) I dreamed I met a fairy who granted me three _____ _____ _____.

10. Every night after we eat I load the dishes into the _____ _____ _____ _____ _____ _____ _____.

In math, we add, subtract, multiply, and div _____.

At the beach, I got stung by a jellyf _____.

Related Words

h _____   w _____ _____ _____

h _____ _____   w

d _____ _____

w _____ _____

d _____ _____ _____ w _____ _____ _____

Rhymes

d _____ _____   w

w _____ _____

h _____ _____

h _____ _____ _____ _____ _____ _____

Name _____

a	e	m	r	s	s	t	t

Make Words

1. Last night, I _____ five pieces of pizza.
2. In _____ class, we paint, draw, and make things.
3. (Add 1 letter.) Let's go shopping at Wal-_____.
4. (Add 1 letter.) He is very _____ and gets all A's.
5. (Change 1 letter.) The game will _____ in five minutes.
6. Texas is a very big _____.
7. (Move the letters.) Can I have a little _____ of your ice cream?
8. What's the m___tt_____ with you?
9. We bought a new m_____ss for my bed.
10. (Move the letters.) He always knew the answers, and everyone agreed he was the _____ person in our class.

Related Words

s _____

s _____

Rhymes

a _____

_____ a _____

Someone left the g_____ open and the dog got out.
The eye doctor had me read the letters on the ch_____.

Lesson 1

13

Name _____

a	e	e	i	c	r	t	y

Make Words

1. The _____ meowed all night.
2. (Move the letters.) She wants to _____ in the play.
3. Yesterday, I a_____ lunch at my grandma's house.
4. (Add 1 letter.) His heart was beating at a very fast r_____.
5. Sometimes bats live in a c_____.
6. (Add 1 letter.) If you really want some ice cream, we could say
   that you _____ _____ _____.
7. (Change 1 letter.) They opened the big _____ _____ _____ the ice cream.
   and took out the bike.
8. (Add 1 letter.) If you make something, we can say that you
   _____ _____ _____ it.
9. It is safe to be here because that volcano is not act _____.
10. If you have lots of good ideas and can create new things, we say
    that you are very _____ _____ _____.

Related Words

a _____

a _____ _____ _____

c _____ _____ _____

c _____ _____ _____ _____

Rhymes

a _____

_____ _____ _____

_____ _____ _____

c _____ _____ _____

c _____ _____ _____

We are going to decor _____ the room for the birthday party.
If you don't beh _____, I will send you to your room.

Lesson 2

Name _____

a	a	e	u	c	h	p	r	t

Make Words

1. Wash your hands and get ready to _____ lunch.

2. (Add 1 letter.) When it gets cold, we turn on the _____ _____.

3. (Change the last letter.) His toys were in a _____ _____ in the corner of his room.

4. (Add 1 letter.) I bought this on sale and it was very _____ _____.

5. (Move the letters.) For dessert, we had _____ _____ pie.

6. (Change the first letter.) Put these scissors up where the baby can't _____ _____ them.

7. (Change the first letter.) Her uncle is going to _____ _____ her to drive.

8. We live on E _____ _____, one of the nine planets.

9. I am reading the last ch _____ _____ of a very good book.

10. The marine put on his _____ _____ and _____ _____ jumped out of the plane.

Rhymes

e _____ _____

_____ _____ _____

h _____ _____

_____ _____ _____

p _____ _____ _____

_____ _____ _____

Soak that shirt in bl _____ and the stains will come out.

The horse can l _____ over the fence.

Lesson 3

Name _____

a	e	i	i	c	s	t	v

Make Words

1. One of my jobs is to _____ the table for dinner.

2. (Change the first letter.) I took my cat to the _____ for his shots.

3. We will e_____ lunch at Grandma's house.

4. Grandma's _____ will get in my lap and purr.

5. (Add 1 letter.) When I want my cat to go away, I will tell him to _____ _____ .

6. (Change 1 letter.) I had a front row s_____ at the game.

7. I am going to s_____ all my money, so I can buy a bike.

8. (Change the first letter.) We crawled into a _____ _____ in the mountain.

9. On Sunday, we drive around and v_____ our relatives.

10. The dentist checked my teeth and happily told me that I had no _____ .

Rhymes

s _____

s _____ _____

c _____   e _____

c _____ _____   _____ _____

s _____ _____

The j_____ got a fl_____ tire and crashed.

Some br_____ people rescued the passengers.

Lesson 4

Name _____

16

a	i	i	c	l	n	p	p	r

Make Words

1. The cat sat in my _____ and began to purr.

2. (Change 1 letter.) I fell and cut my _____ .

3. (Add 1 letter.) Use a paper _____ to hold those papers together.

4. (Change 1 letter.) When the concert ended, everyone began to _____ .

5. Pound this n_____ into the wall so we can hang this picture.

6. (Change the first letter.) She carried the water in a _____ .

7. (Change the last letter.) I fell on the ice and now I have a _____ in my back.

8. (Add 1 letter.) I like _____ clothes, but my sister likes fancy clothes.

9. If there is a fire, you should try not to p_____ c!

10. The head of our school is called the _____ .

Rhymes

l _____ — ——

—— —— ——

—— —— ——

n —— —— ——

—— —— ——

l —— —— ——

—— —— ——

p —— —— ——

The tr____ led to a cabin in the woods.

It was snowing hard, so we decided to rem____ there until morning.

Lesson 5

17

Name _____

e	i	o	u	n	q	s	s	t

Make Words

1. The boy had to t ____ his little brother's shoes.
2. The theater was almost full, and we had to ____ in the last row.
3. My mom q____ her job and is looking for another one.
4. Write your mother a n____ and tell her when you will be home.
5. (Change 1 letter.) We use our ____ to smell things.
6. Be very q____, so you don't wake the baby.
7. (Move the letters.) I am not q____ ready to go.
8. (Change 1 letter.) When you report someone's exact words, you have a ____.
9. (opposite of #1) Can you help me ____ ____ this knot?
10. Does anyone want to ask any more ____ ____?

Related Words

t ____

t ____

Rhymes

s ____

____ ____

n ____

____ ____

Use the rem____ control to change the channels.
The criminal would not adm____ that he was guilty.

Lesson 6

Name ____

e	e	i	d	h	r	s	v

Make Words

1. The stripes on our flag are ___ ___ ___ and white.
2. (Change 1 letter.) Let's get ___ ___ ___ of all these old clothes.
3. (Change 1 letter.) The boy ___ ___ ___ behind the garage.
4. (Add 1 letter.) They were playing ___ ___ ___ ___ and seek.
5. (Change 1 letter.) Bees live in a ___ ___ ___ ___.
6. (Change the first letter.) I am going to ___ ___ ___ ___ into the pool.
7. (Add 1 letter.) I want to be the best ___ ___ ___ ___ ___ on the Olympic team.
8. (Move the letters.) He will ___ ___ ___ ___ ___ the bus to the game.
9. When it is very cold, sometimes your body will shake and sh ___ ___ ___ ___ ___.
10. (Add 2 letters.) The heat in the truck wasn't working, and we ___ ___ ___ ___ ___ ___ all the way home.

Related Words

h ___ ___ ___ ___   d ___ ___ ___ ___

h ___ ___ ___ ___   d ___ ___ ___ ___

sh ___ ___ ___ ___

sh ___ ___ ___ ___

Rhymes

r ___ ___ ___   h ___ ___ ___ ___

___ ___ ___   ___ ___ ___ ___

___ ___ ___ ___   ___ ___ ___ ___

The stranded people had to surv___ without food or water for three days. I wonder how the Egyptians could build that huge pyram___.

Lesson 7

Name ___

e	e	i	o	n	p	p	p	r

Make Words

1. The lady wore a pretty p_____ on her jacket.
2. (Move the letters.) The puppy began to _____ at my toes.
3. (Change 1 letter.) When I open a present, I _____ _____ the paper off the box.
4. (Add 1 letter.) We pick the fruit when it is _____ _____.
5. (Change 1 letter.) The old man rocked and smoked his _____.
6. The stores will _____ _____ at 10:00.
7. (Add 2 letters.) I will open this with the can _____ _____.
8. Please pass the salt and _____ _____.
9. The p_____ _____ went west in a covered wagon.
10. Do you like _____ _____ on your pizza?

Related Words

o _____ _____

o _____ _____

p _____

p _____ _____ _____

Rhymes

n _____ _____

_____ _____ _____

p _____ _____

_____ _____

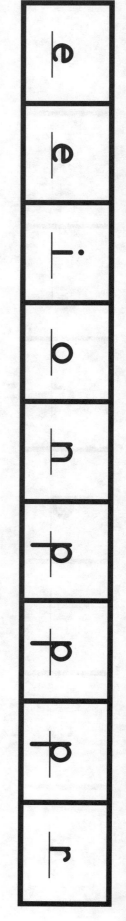

Get a sponge and w_____ off the tables.
The aliens arrived in a spacesh_____.

Lesson 8

Name _____

a	a	i	o	d	l	r	r	s

Make Words

1. Every four months, my dad changes the o_____ in our car.
2. (Add 1 letter.) To grow, plants need food, water, and good _____.
3. (Change 1 letter.) This is a good day to _____ our boat.
4. (Change 1 letter.) The old man held on to the _____ as he went up the steps.
5. We had to take a detour because the r_____ was under construction.
6. (Change 1 letter.) The truck delivered a _____ of wood for the fire.
7. She turned on the r_____ and heard her favorite song.
8. The police were using r_____ to find the speeding cars.
9. We call someone who is in the navy a s_____.
10. It is very hard work laying the track that built the _____.

Related Words

s_____

s_____

r_____

r_____

r_____ r_____

Rhymes

o_____

_____

r_____ _____

r_____

The robbers were arrested and put in j_____.
Put that food in the refrigerator so it won't sp_____.

Name _____

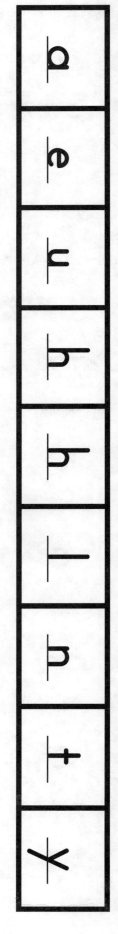

| a | e | u | h | h | t | n | t | y |

Make Words

1. I stayed _____ my cousin's house.
2. (Add 1 letter.) Yesterday, I _____ _____ apple pie for dessert.
3. (Move the letters.) Come and _____ _____ lunch.
4. (Add 1 letter.) When it is cold we turn on the _____ _____.
5. (Change the first letter.) My room is clean and _____ _____.
6. If you are not on time, you are _____ _____.
7. (Change the first letter.) Some people like spinach, but other people _____ _____ it.
8. After my checkup, the doctor told me that I was in very good _____.
9. (Add 1 letter.) I felt even better knowing that I was very _____.
10. (opposite of #9) Many people in poor countries do not have good food or water and are very _____.

First, we are going to sk _____.
Then, we are going to have a tr _____.

Related Words

h _____ _____ _____
h _____ _____ _____
h _____ _____ _____

Rhymes

a _____
_____ _____
_____ _____
e _____
_____ _____
_____ _____

e	e	o	h	m	p	s	r	t	t

Make Words

1. I had to study for my spelling _____.

2. (Change 1 letter.) My little brother ate all the _____ of the cookies.

3. (Change 1 letter.) Sometimes my little brother is a real _____.

4. (Move the letters.) The baby took his first _____ when he was 10 months old.

5. (Add 1 letter.) It was hard work pedaling up the _____ hill.

6. (Change 1 letter.) We get wool from _____.

7. The opposite of tall is _____.

8. (Change 1 letter.) Soccer is a very popular _____.

9. The children went to the grocery store with their _____.

10. (Add 4 letters.) The children live with their father and his wife, who is their _____.

Related Words

_____ m _____

_____ m _____

Rhymes

_____ t _____

s _____ _____ _____

_____ _____ _____

_____ s _____

I wrote a rep_____ on whales for my science class.

The police told the robber that he was under arr_____.

Lesson 11

Name _____

e	e	i	b	g	n	n	r	s

Make Words

1. He got stung by a _____ _____.

2. (Change 1 letter.) I can _____ _____ _____ a lot better with my new glasses.

3. (Add 1 letter.) Have you _____ _____ _____ the new movie?

4. Next year I am going to _____ _____ in the choir.

5. (Change 1 letter.) The bells will _____ _____ _____ at midnight.

6. (Add 1 letter.) I will come to the party and _____ _____ _____ some cookies.

7. What time will the party b_____ _____ _____?

8. Stop when the light is red and go when it turns _____ _____ _____.

9. The _____ _____ _____ _____ is the first car on the train.

10. The YMCA has swimming classes for advanced swimmers and _____ _____ _____ who are just learning for _____ _____ _____ how to swim.

Related Words

s _____   s _____ .

b _____   s _____

b _____ _____ _____ _____

Rhymes

b _____

s _____ _____   s _____ _____

s _____ _____ _____   s _____ _____ _____

The number six comes betw _____ the numbers five and seven.

The fans booed the refer _____ when they thought he wasn't being fair.

Lesson 12

Name _____

e	i	d	d	h	l	l	n	s	w

Make Words

1. I _____ my homework as soon as I got home.
2. (Change 1 letter.) The scared cat _____ under the bed.
3. (Add 1 letter.) That is the cat's favorite place to _____ _____ .
4. (Change 1 letter.) We walked down the right _____ _____ of the road.
5. (Change 1 letter.) The opposite of narrow is _____ .
6. During the storm, the _____ _____ blew at 50 miles an hour.
7. The children climbed the ladder and slid down the _____ _____ .
8. The key was _____ under the mat.
9. It is cold outside, but it is warm _____ by the fire.
10. As we were driving down the dirt road, a rock flew up and cracked our _____ _____ .

Related Words

h _____ _____

h _____ _____

h _____ _____

w _____ _____

w _____ _____

Rhymes

d _____

h _____

_____ _____

_____ _____

In math, we are learning to multiply and div_____ .

The part of your eye that you close is your eyel_____ .

Lesson 13

Name _____

e	e	i	o	l	m	s	t	t

Make Words

1. When you don't tell the truth, you are telling a _____ _____ _____.

2. (Change 1 letter.) When I was little, I didn't know how to _____ _____ _____ _____ my shoes.

3. (Add 1 letter.) What _____ _____ _____ _____ is it?

4. (Change 1 letter.) Have you ever had _____ _____ _____ _____ sherbet?

5. (Move the letters.) One grandma lives a _____ _____ _____ _____ away.

6. (Add 1 letter.) My other grandma lives 100 _____ _____ _____ _____ away.

7. (Move the letters.) When you have your picture taken, you are supposed to _____ _____ _____ _____.

8. (Move the letters.) There was a lot of green _____ _____ _____ _____ at the bottom of the swimming pool.

9. On our trip, we stayed at a m _____ _____ _____ with a swimming pool.

10. At Christmas, you are supposed to kiss someone who stands under the _____ _____ _____ _____ _____ _____ _____ _____ _____.

Have you ever seen a crocod _____ _____ _____ ?
Did you know it is a rept _____ _____ ?

Rhymes

l _____ _____

_____ _____ _____
_____ _____ _____

t _____ _____ _____

m _____ _____ _____

_____ _____ _____

Lesson 14

Name _____

26

a	e	i	o	o	g	l	p	z

Make Words

1. On Saturday, we will all _____ to see the movie.

2. (Add 1 letter.) My great-grandma was born a long time _____.

3. We took a trip to the _____ and saw all kinds of animals.

4. When it is cold, I z_____ up my jacket.

5. (Change the first letter.) I fell off my bike and cut my _____.

6. Put another _____ on the fire.

7. (Change 1 letter.) He had a skiing accident and broke his _____.

8. They raised the a_____ when you can get a driver's license from 16 to 17.

9. (Add 1 letter.) The teacher asked us to open our books to _____ 36.

10. When you _____, you say you are sorry for what you did.

Rhymes

z _____ _____

_____ _____ _____

a _____

_____ _____ _____

Our class took a field tr_____ to the zoo.

The band was on st_____ and ready to begin the concert.

Lesson 15

Name _____

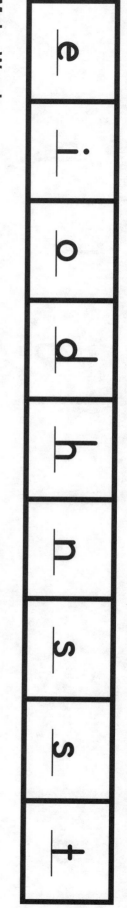

| e | i | o | d | h | n | s | s | t |

Make Words

1. A story has a beginning, middle, and ―――――― ――――――.
2. (Add 1 letter.) When I get there, I will ―――――― ―――――― you a postcard.
3. My mom wrote a n―――――― to the teacher.
4. (Change 1 letter.) An elephant's ―――――― is called a trunk.
5. (Change 1 letter.) We used the ―――――― to water the plants.
6. (Move the letters.) Can you help me find my other ―――――― plants.
7. The d―――――― ――――――? broke when I dropped it on the floor.
8. (Add 2 letters.) I was more careful when I picked up the other ―――――― ―――――― ――――――.
9. An h―――――― person does not lie, cheat, or steal.
10. (opposite of #9) We didn't trust him because he was ―――――― ――――――.

The coach ch―――――― the best players to be on the team.
Let's pret―――――― we are traveling to another planet.

Related Words

d ― ―――――― ――――――
d ―――――― ――――――

h ―――――― ――――――
h ―――――― ――――――

Rhymes

e ――――――
―――――― ――――――
―――――― ――――――
n ―――――― ――――――
―――――― ――――――

Name ――――――

e	i	o	c	d	r	s	v	y

Make Words

1. I have to go home and _____ my homework.

2. The baby will c_____ when she is hungry.

3. (Change 1 letter.) I will wash the dishes and you can _____ them.

4. It is fun to d_____ into the pool.

5. (Add 1 letter.) When I am older, I will be able to _____ the car.

6. The baby c_____ when his mother left.

7. (Change 2 letters.) I wash the dishes and she _____ them.

8. Put the c_____ on the pan, and the food will stay hot.

9. (Add 3 letters.) The explorers set out to _____ new lands.

10. (Add 1 letter.) The scientist made an amazing _____.

Related Words

d_____   c_____

d_____   c_____

c_____

c_____

c_____

Rhymes

c_____   c_____

d_____

d_____

The robber used a screwdriver to p_____ open the door.
We waited at the airport for the plane to arr_____.

Lesson 17

29

Name _____

e	o	o	g	n	r	r	s	y

Make Words

1. I am going to ask my mom if I can _____ to the mall.

2. (Add 2 letters.) My friend _____ to the mall every week.

3. (Change 2 letters.) Have you ever _____ to the mall?

4. Our pitcher can't pitch today because she has a _____ arm.

5. (Move the letters.) We have a beautiful red _____ bush in our yard.

6. (Change the first letter.) I have a stuffy _____ .

7. (Add 1 letter.) The loop at the end of a lasso is called a _____ .

8. (Change the first letter.) A _____ looks like a duck, but is bigger and has a longer neck.

9. The job of the president and congress is to g_____ the country.

10. The _____ of the 50 states held a meeting to discuss the problems of pollution and the environment.

These jeans fit before I lost 20 pounds, but now they are too l_____ .
Turn on the h_____ and let's wash the car.

Related Words

g_____

g_____

g_____

Rhymes

g_____

n_____

n_____

n_____

Name _____

e	e	o	l	p	r	s	s	w

Make Words

1. I fell and sprained my wrist, and it is very _____.

2. (Move the letters.) The man went to the flower shop and bought his girlfriend one beautiful red _____.

3. (Change 1 letter.) When you _____ something, you have to find it.

4. The robber _____ a mask over his face.

5. When you cry very quietly, you _____.

6. (Add 1 letter.) One of my jobs is to _____ the floor.

7. (Change 1 letter.) The baby went to _____ at 7:00.

8. The p_____ was off at our house for three days after the tornado.

9. When we win, we are the winners but when we lose, we are the _____.

10. When you don't have the power to do anything, you are _____.

Related Words

l _____

l _____

p _____

p _____

Rhymes

s _____

_____

w _____

_____

We drove the j_____ to the grocery st_____.

Lesson 19

Name _____

a	e	e	c	g	h	l	l	n

Make Words

Rhymes

1. My sister ate _____ the cookies and didn't save any!

2. How old you are is your _____.

3. (Add 1 letter.) The birds were living in a large _____ _____.

4. Can I use your phone to _____ _____ my mom?

5. (Change 1 letter.) The class walked quietly down the _____ _____ to the gym.

6. The bald _____ le is the national bird of the United States.   a _____

7. (Change 2 letters.) Can you find the largest _____ _____ of that triangle?   _____ _____
_____ _____
_____ _____

8. (Move the letters.) Some people put an _____ _____ _____ on top of their Christmas tree.   a _____
_____ _____

9. Do you mind if I ch _____ _____ the channel?

10. Winning the game without our star player was a real _____ _____ _____ for our team, but they did it!

On Friday night, we all go to the footb _____ game.
The actors all came out on st _____, and the audience clapped and clapped.

Name _____

a	e	i	o	c	c	⊥	m	m	r

Make Words

1. She had two scoops of chocolate ____ ____ cream.
2. (Add 1 letter.) Our cat likes to chase ____ ____.
3. (Change 1 letter.) Do you like fried ____ ____?
4. (Change 1 letter.) The fastest runner will win the ____ ____.
5. (Change 1 letter.) Her dress was trimmed with ____ ____.
6. (Change 1 letter.) The horse couldn't run because her leg was ____ ____.
7. (Move the letters.) He went to McDonald's® and got his favorite ____ ____.
8. (Change 1 letter.) Those artificial flowers look very ____ ____.
9. We went to the cookout to celebrate M ____ ____ Day.
10. I was watching a movie on TV and at the best part, they stopped the movie for a ____ ____ ____.

Rhymes

i ____ ____

____ ____ ____

____ ____ ____

m ____ ____

____ ____ ____

r ____ ____

____ ____ ____

This movie will app ____ ____ to people of all ages.

Last summer, my family visited the birthpl ____ ____ of George Washington.

Lesson 21

33

Name ____

a	e	e	i	d	g	r	s

Make Words

1. When my dog died, I felt very ___ ___ ___.
2. This shirt has holes in it and can only be used as a dust ___ ___ ___.
3. (Add 1 letter.) It took two big men to ___ ___ ___ ___ the heavy box in the garage.
4. (Move the letters.) When you graduate, we call you a ___ ___ ___.
5. This weekend I am going to ___ ___ ___ ___ this whole book.
6. (Move the letters.) I started my letter with the greeting,
"___ ___ ___ ___ Mr. Green."
7. Mrs. Brown teaches the fourth ___ ___ ___ ___ ___.
8. It was hard to get everyone to ag ___ ___ ___ on where we could eat.
9. (Add 1 letter.) Finally, everyone ___ ___ ___ ___ ___ to eat at Taco Bell®.
10. (opposite of #8) Usually we agree, but sometimes we ___ ___ ___ ___ ___.

Related Words

a ___ ___

___ ___ ___ a ___ ___

Rhymes

s ___ ___

___ ___ ___

r ___ ___

___ ___ ___

I am the fastest runner but I try not to br ___ ___ too much about it.
I went fishing with my grandd ___ ___ ___.

© Carson-Dellosa CD-2611

Lesson 22

Name _____

e	i	b	g	h	r	s	t	t

Make Words

1. The batter _____ the ball out of the park.

2. I am tired and am going to r _____ for awhile.

3. (Change 1 letter.) My grandma makes the very _____ cookies.

4. The blind man lost his _____ in an accident.

5. (Change the first letter.) My house is the large white one on the _____ side of the street.

6. In the *Winnie the Pooh* books, Tigger is a _____.

7. The person who hits the ball is called the _____.

8. (Change 1 letter.) The four tastes are sweet, sour, salty, and _____.

9. It is a clear night and the stars are very _____.

10. (Add 3 letters.) The _____ planet in the sky is Venus.

Related Words

h _____

h _____

b _____

b _____

Rhymes

b _____

r _____

h _____

_____

When my parents go out, they pay me to be the babys _____.
I made the best poster and won the cont _____.

Lesson 23

35

Name _____

e	i	o	b	g	h	n	r	s

Make Words

1. I turned on the radio and they were playing my favorite
   __ __ __ __ __ .

2. (Change 1 letter.) When I grow up, I want to __ __ __ __ in a
   band.

3. (Change 1 letter.) I was on my way out when the phone started to
   __ __ __ __ .

4. The man jumped in the freezing water to save the baby and
   everyone said he was a __ __ __ __ .

5. Abraham Lincoln was __ __ __ __ on February 22.

6. (Change 1 letter.) "Little Boy Blue, come blow your
   __ __ __ __ ."

7. We went to the ranch, and I rode my uncle's __ __ __ __ __ .

8. Dogs like to chew on __ __ __ __ __ .

9. Elvis Presley was a famous rock and roll __ __ __ __ __ .

10. The people who live in our neighborhood are called our
    __ __ __ __ __ __ __ __ .

I always eat popc_____ at the movies.
We were bored and couldn't think of anyth_____ to do.

Related Words

s __ __ __ __

s __ __ __ __

s __ __ __ __ __ __

Rhymes

s __ __ __

__ __ __ __

__ __ __ __

b __ __ __

__ __ __ __

i	o	o	u	l	l	n	p	t

Make Words

1. What time is ___ ___ ___ ___ ?
2. (Add 1 letter.) When the power went off, we ___ ___ candles.
3. (Change 1 letter.) The seed of a peach is called a ___ ___ ___ .
4. On hot days, I swim in my friend's swimming ___ ___ ___ ___ .
5. (Change 1 letter.) Please get my hammer from the ___ ___ ___ ___ box.
6. Once ___ ___ ___ ___ a time, there were three little pigs.
7. I have to wait here u ___ ___ ___ ___ my mom gets home.
8. The ___ ___ ___ ___ ___ is the person who flies the airplane.
9. To be sure we don't get a sunburn, we put suntan ___ ___ ___ ___ ___ on before we go outside.
10. All cars have to be inspected to make sure they are not causing too much air ___ ___ ___ ___ ___ ___ ___ .

Rhymes

i ___

___ ___ ___
___ ___ ___
___ ___ ___

p ___ ___ ___
___ ___ ___

The criminal never did adm ___ ___ ___ that he had committed the crime.
We are moving and I will go to a new sch ___ ___ ___ next year.

Lesson 25

Name ___

e	e	i	d	h	p	r	s	w

Make Words

1. When it is very hot, we like to take a quick d_____ in the pool.
2. (Change the first letter.) My grandma fell and broke her _____.
3. (Add 1 letter.) The sailors sailed away on a giant _____ _____.
4. Brian's mom came looking for him, but I told her he was not _____.
5. (Change 1 letter.) A new factory is being built and they will _____ _____ a lot of people.
6. (Change 1 letter.) They put up a large _____ _____ fence around the building.
7. On my birthday, I blow out the candles and make a _____ _____.
8. (Add 2 letters.) One year, I _____ _____ _____ for a new bike and got one!
9. When you want to tell someone a secret, you should _____ _____ it, so no one else can hear.
10. (Add 2 letters.) My friend _____ _____ a _____ secret to me.

My uncle says he is going to ret_____ and move to Florida.

We will take a tr_____ and go visit him.

Related Words

w_____

w_____

w_____ _____ _____

w_____ _____ _____

Rhymes

h_____ _____

d_____ _____

_____ _____ _____

_____ _____ _____

Lesson 26

Name _____

a	a	i	c	f	n	s	t	t

Make Words

1. When it is hot, we turn on the _____.

2. (Change 1 letter.) I opened a _____ of soup and heated it for lunch.

3. (Change 1 letter.) My pet is a Siamese _____.

4. (Change 1 letter.) My cat eats too much and is getting _____.

5. (Add 1 letter.) The race car could go very _____.

6. We had just one cat, but we adopted some others and now we have seven _____.

7. (Move the letters.) She broke her arm and had a _____ on it.

8. (Move the letters.) My sister _____ in lots of plays.

9. (Add 1 letter.) I know a lot of _____ about snakes.

10. The movie we saw last night was absolutely _____.

Related Words

f _____

_____

Rhymes

c _____   f _____

_____

_____

a _____   f _____

_____

The parade went right p _____ my house.

I like to read Batm _____ and Superm _____ comic books.

Lesson 27

Name _____

| a | e | o | u | d | g | n | r | s |

Make Words

1. Ask your dad if you can _____ to the mall.

2. (Add 2 letters.) My friend _____ _____ _____ to the mall every Saturday.

3. We hear with our _____.

4. (Add 1 letter.) When you drive a dump truck, you have to shift _____ _____ _____.

5. We crept quietly into the house trying not to make a s_____ _____ _____.

6. (Change the first letter.) A circle is _____ _____ _____ _____.

7. (Add 1 letter.) We were going the wrong way, so we had to turn _____ _____ _____ _____.

8. (Change 1 letter.) It snowed last night, and the _____ _____ _____ _____ is covered in snow .

9. When the river flooded, the people living nearby were in great _____ _____ _____ _____.

10. (Add 3 letters.) Power lines came down, and it was _____ _____ _____ _____ _____ _____ to walk or drive.

Related Words

g _____

g _____ _____ _____

d _____ _____ _____

d _____ _____ _____ _____

Rhymes

e _____ _____

_____ _____ _____

s _____ _____ _____

_____ _____ _____ _____

_____ _____ _____ _____

The score was tied when our center got a reb_____ and scored a goal.
When my dog comes in, my cat disapp_____.

Name _____

a	e	f	n	r	r	s	t

Make Words

1. We drove to the store because it was too _____ to walk.

2. (Add 1 letter.) Some people have a terrible f_____ of snakes.

3. (Change the first letter.) I wished my friend still lived _____ me.

4. The mother bird had three baby birds in her _____.

5. (Change the first letter.) I ate the _____ of the cook-ies.

6. Look at the bright _____ in the sky.

7. (Add 1 letter.) People don't like it when you st_____ at them.

8. Ten is the number that comes _____ nine.

9. I will win the race because I can run _____ than you can.

10. You may have to _____ to a new school when you move.

Rhymes

f_____

_____ _____

f_____ _____

_____ _____

n_____ _____

_____ _____

Last y_____, we drove our old c_____ w_____ to California.

Name_____

a	a	e	e	h	l	r	r	s

Make Words

1. The old man can't hear very well with his left _____.

2. (Add 1 letter.) He can _____ _____ fine with his right ear.

3. (Change the last letter.) My arm was very sore until the wound began to _____.

4. (Change the first letter.) I'm not scared of movie monsters because I know they are not _____ _____ _____.

5. (Change the first letter.) At the water show, we watched a _____ _____ _____.

6. Put the l _____ _____ catch a ball with his flippers.

7. When I have a snack, I sh _____ _____ it with my friend.

8. Could you please e _____ _____ the board?

9. (Add 1 letter.) I will erase the board, but I can't find the _____ _____ _____.

10. Tonight, we have a _____ _____ _____ _____ to

For breakfast, sometimes I eat oatm _____.

The magician made the rabbit disapp _____.

Related Words

e _____ _____ _____

e _____ _____ _____

Rhymes

e _____ _____

e _____ _____

r _____ _____

_____ _____ _____

a	e	i	u	n	q	t	s

Make Words

1. I'm hungry and want something good to _____.
2. I am teaching my little brother to _____ his shoes.
3. The bus driver told everyone to _____ down and be quiet.
4. (Add 1 letter.) The place where a building is being built is called the building _____.
5. The opposite of sloppy is _____.
6. My dad is going to _____ his job because he has found a better one.
7. (Add 1 letter.) The cake is not _____ done yet.
8. (Move the letters.) Sometimes the teacher tells us to be _____ _____.
9. (opposite of #2) My shoelace has a knot in it and I can't _____ _____ it.
10. My aunt runs a store where she sells old furniture, dishes, jewelry, and other _____.

Related Words

t _____
t _____

Rhymes

e _____
s _____
s _____

We don't need cable because we get our TV channels through a satell_____ dish.
I don't see how anyone can mistr_____ an animal.

Lesson 31

Name _____

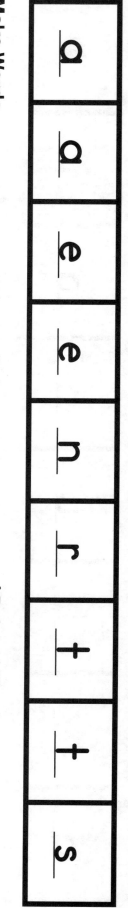

| a | a | e | e | n | r | t | t | s |

Make Words

1. When lunch was ready, Mom called everyone to come and _____.

2. (Add 1 letter.) When we go on trips, my brother and I argue about who gets the front _____ _____ _____.

3. (Change 1 letter.) My room is always messy, but my brother's room is always _____ _____ _____.

4. We were having a picnic when a bunch of tiny black _____ started crawling all over the blanket.

5. When we camp out, we sleep in a _____.

6. (Change 1 letter.) The _____ for our apartment is $500.00 a month.

7. My cat is sick and hasn't e_____ _____ any food for three days.

8. My brother's room is neat, but my sister's room is even _____ _____ _____.

9. I want my room to be the _____ room of all.

10. Animals with long noses that eat ants are called _____ _____ _____.

Related Words

a _____

a _____ — _____ — _____

n _____ — e

n _____ — e

n _____ — _____ — e

Rhymes

e _____ — _____

e _____ — r _____ — _____

I am working on an experim_____ for the science fair.

I want to inv_____ something no one has ever thought of.

Name _____

i	i	u	b	f	g	g	h	l	l	n	t

Make Words

1. Every month, we have to pay the electric b _____ _____.

2. (Change 1 letter.) A male cow is called a _____ _____.

3. (Change 1 letter.) The opposite of empty is _____ _____.

4. When we take a test, we have to _____ _____ _____ in the little circles next to the right answers.

5. The two boys got mad at each other and started to _____ _____ _____.

6. (Change 1 letter.) My friend and I play video games every Friday _____ _____ _____.

7. (Change 1 letter.) When it gets dark, we turn on the _____ _____ _____.

8. (Add 1 letter.) Wilbur and Orville Wright took the first _____ _____ _____ airplane _____ _____ _____.

9. My sister and I are always f _____ _____ _____ over who gets the remote.

10. (Add 4 letters.) _____ _____ _____ _____ is a popular sport in Spain, but it is very dangerous.

Related Words

f _____ _____

f _____ _____

b _____ _____

b _____ _____

b _____ _____

Rhymes

b _____ _____   b _____ _____

_____ _____ n _____

_____ _____ _____

_____ _____ _____

_____ _____ _____

Seeing my favorite singer in person was quite a thr _____ _____ _____. We ride down on our sleds and then p _____ _____ _____ them back up the hill.

Lesson 33

45

Name _____

e	o	u	b	d	l	l	r	s	z

Make Words

1. The opposite of new is _____.
2. (Add 1 letter.) Another word for brave is _____.
3. I am saving my money, and my cousin is going to _____ me his old bike.
4. (Change 1 letter.) When the _____ rings, we have to be in our classroom.
5. (Change 1 letter.) A male cow is called a _____.
6. Sometimes, I have to turn the music down because it is too _____.
7. I have a sister who is younger than me and a sister who is _____ than me.
8. I listen to loud music and my sister likes to turn it up even _____.
9. The twins were always getting into things, so we called them d_____ _____ trouble.
10. Large tractors that move rocks and trees are called _____.

I couldn't see because my eyes were covered with a blindf_____.
My mother has a new c_____ phone.

Related Words

o — — —
o — — — — —
l — — — —

b — — —
b — — —

Rhymes

b — — —
— — —
— — —

o — —
— — —
— — —

Lesson 34

Name _____

a	a	e	i	c	c	d	l	n	t

Make Words

1. Last night, I _____ two pieces of chocolate cake.
2. (Add 1 letter.) We hurry in the morning, so we won't be _____ for school.
3. (Move the letters.) Snow White is a fairy ___ ___ ___ ___.
4. (sounds like #3) My dog wags his ___ ___ ___.
5. (Change 1 letter.) Can you hammer this ___ ___ ___ ___ into the wall for me?
6. We call a creature from another planet an ___ ___ ___ ___ ___.
7. After the football game, we had a d ___ ___ ___ ___ in the gym.
8. It was raining so hard, they had to c ___ ___ ___ ___ ___ the game.
9. My sister said I broke the lamp on purpose, but it was an a ___ ___ ___ ___ ___ ___ ___.
10. (Add 2 letters.) When something is an accident, we say it was ___ ___ ___ ___ ___ ___ ___ ___.

Related Words

a ___ ___ ___ ___ ___ ___ ___

a ___ ___ ___ ___ ___ ___ ___

Rhymes

a ___ ___

n ___ ___ ___ ___

A train that goes on one track is called a monor ___ ___ ___.

My uncle only speaks Spanish, so my mom has to transl ___ ___ ___ what he says because she is the only one in the family who speaks Spanish.

Lesson 35

Name _____

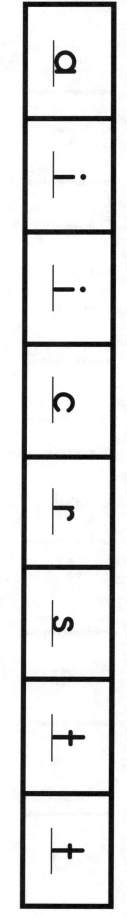

a	i	i	c	r	s	t	t

Make Words

1. We rode to the mall in my dad's new _____.

2. (Change 1 letter.) My _____ meows every time we leave her.

3. (Change 1 letter.) A _____ is a rodent, but is bigger than a mouse.

4. (Move the letters.) We painted some great pictures in _____ class.

5. (Add 1 letter.) When we go to the store, I push the grocery _____.

6. Our sun is a very big and very bright _____.

7. (Add 1 letter.) Do you know what time the game will _____?

8. Our teacher is very s_____ and makes sure everyone follows the rules.

9. A person who draws, paints, or sculpts is called an _____.

10. (Add 2 letters.) We say someone who is good at art is very _____.

Related Words

a _____

a _____

a _____

Rhymes

c _____   c _____

c _____   a _____

Michael Jordan was a basketball superst_____.

The place were an animal lives is called its habit_____.

Lesson 36

© Carson-Dellosa CD-2611

Name _____

48

a	a	e	e	b	c	c	l	p	t

Make Words

1. Yesterday, I _____ lunch at my grandma's house.

2. (Change 1 letter.) President Lincoln's first name was _____.

3. (Add 1 letter.) My grandpa hurt his leg and is not _____ to walk.

4. I try to get home on time because my mom gets mad if I am _____.

5. (Add 1 letter.) I was hungry, so I filled my _____ with food.

6. One of my jobs is to set the _____ for dinner.

7. (Change 1 letter.) We get lots of channels because we have _____ TV.

8. The king and queen lived in a beautiful _____.

9. We tried to give her some money, but she wouldn't acc_____ it.

10. (Add 4 letters.) My teacher said that my homework was not perfect, but that it was _____.

Related Words

a _____

a _____

Rhymes

a _____

a _____

The horses and cows lived in a st_____.

Some birds migr_____ south in the winter.

Lesson 37

Name _____

49

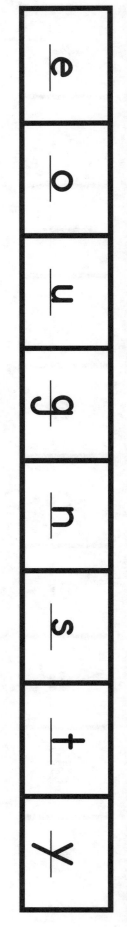

Make Words

1. The opposite of no is ___.

2. When I get a new bike, I will give my old one to y___.

3. Squirrels eat the ___ that fall from the trees.

4. (Change 1 letter.) The parts of your body inside your belly are called your ___ ___ ___.

5. (Change 1 letter.) I hope my sister ___ ___ ___ a computer game for her birthday.

6. (Change 1 letter.) The fishermen caught fish in big ___ ___ ___.

7. (Move the letters.) The mama bird made a ___ ___ ___ for her eggs.

8. A person who comes to visit you is called your gu ___ ___.

9. The opposite of old is ___ ___ ___.

10. (Add 3 letters.) I am the ___ ___ ___ ___ child in our family.

Related Words

y ___ ___ ___

y ___ ___ ___ ___

Rhymes

n ___ ___

g ___ ___ ___

n ___ ___ ___

My dad took all three of us to the barbershop to get hairc___.

The policeman told the robber that she was under arr___.

Name ___

e	i	i	f	i	r	r	t	z
e	e	i	f	i	r	r	t	z

Make Words

1. On our trip, we had to stop and fix a flat _____.

2. (Change 1 letter.) There used to be a house there, but it was destroyed in the _____.

3. All those leaves fell off that big _____.

4. (Change 1 letter.) Something that doesn't cost anything is _____.

5. (Change 1 letter.) They ran after the man when he started to _____.

6. (Move the letters.) I was sick, but today I _____ much better.

7. (Change 1 letter.) An elephant has four _____.

8. (Add 1 letter.) A large group of ships is called a _____.

9. My grandma is 65 and she is going to r_____ _____ from her job and come live with us.

10. When we plant our garden, we feed the plants with _____.

Rhymes

f _____

_____

_____

f _____

t _____

_____

_____

Our pet parak_____ lives in a cage.
In a baseball game, the ump_____ decides if a pitch is a ball or a strike.

Lesson 39

Name_____

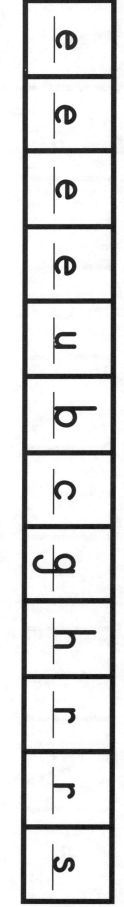

Make Words

1. Another name for an insect is a b ___ ___.

2. (Change 1 letter.) I gave my grandma a big ___ ___ ___.

3. (Add 1 letter.) A word that means really big is ___ ___ ___ ___.

4. We woke up late and had to r ___ ___ ___ to get ready.

5. (Add 1 letter.) Every night, I ___ ___ ___ ___ my teeth.

6. The cheerleaders led the ___ ___ ___ ___ ___ at the game.

7. The little boy fell in the old well and the fire department had to r ___ ___ ___ ___ ___ him.

8. (Move the letters.) We locked all the doors, so the house was safe and ___ ___ ___ ___ ___.

9. Have you ever had a grilled ___ ___ ___ ___ ___ sandwich?

10. (Add 6 letters.) My brother likes a plain hamburger, but I always order a ___ ___ ___ ___ ___ ___ ___ ___ ___ with everything on it.

Related Words

c ___ ___ ___ ___ ___

c ___ ___ ___ ___ ___ ___ ___

Rhymes

b ___ ___

___ ___ ___

r ___ ___

___ ___ ___

___ ___ ___

When we have a bad storm, I always unpl ___ ___ ___ the TV.

My little brother always forgets to fl ___ ___ ___ the toilet.

Lesson 40

Name ___

a	o	g	h	h	p	p	r	s	t

Make Words

1. A _____ is a rodent that is usually bigger than a mouse.
2. (Move the letters.) We painted murals in _____ class.
3. (Add 1 letter.) He had a big _____ in the play.
4. (Move the letters.) The mouse got caught in the _____.
5. (Add 1 letter.) One _____ on my backpack is broken.
6. (Move the letters.) We are having a rehearsal to practice our _____ in the play.
7. Tennis is my favorite _____.
8. (Change 1 letter.) The opposite of tall is _____.
9. We are studying weather and we made g_____phs showing the temperature on different days.
10. (Add 5 letters.) That album with the green cover has all the _____ from our trip.

Related Words

g _____ _____

g _____ _____

Rhymes

a _____ _____

t _____ _____

s _____ _____

_____ _____ _____

The men were arrested when they tried to kidn_____ the baby.

When you travel to other countries, you need a passp_____.

Lesson 41

Name _____

a	e	u	b	l	l	m	r	s

Make Words

1. I am going out to play now because I have finished _____ my homework.

2. (Add 1 letter.) Let's go shopping at the _____ _____.

3. (Add 1 letter.) I need new shoes because these are too _____ _____.

4. When you play a game, it is important to follow the r _____ _____.

5. (Change 1 letter.) _____ _____ _____ are part donkey and part horse.

6. We put all the pictures in our photo a _____ _____ _____.

7. My dad and I are going to get l _____ _____ to build a treehouse.

8. (Move the letters.) We could hear the low r _____ _____ _____ _____ of thunder in the distance.

9. Mosquitoes are small insects, but ants are even _____ _____ _____ _____ _____.

10. When it rains, we stay dry because we walk under our _____ _____ _____ _____.

Related Words

s _____ _____ _____

s _____ _____ _____

Rhymes

a _____

_____ _____ _____

r _____ _____ _____

_____ _____ _____

My friends and I like to play basketb_____.
We also like to play baseb_____ and footb_____.

o	o	u	d	g	g	h	n	r

Make Words

1. Our pet _____ is a 15-year-old collie named Sam.
2. (Change 1 letter.) Another name for a pig is a _____.
3. (Change 1 letter.) Grandma gave me a big _____ before she left.
4. (Change 1 letter.) We _____ a hole in the sand.
5. The opposite of bad is _____.
6. (Change 1 letter.) My jacket has a _____ I can put on my head when it snows.
7. My friend has a h_____ dog that is a very good hunter.
8. (Change 1 letter.) A circle is _____.
9. (Add 1 letter.) The snow covered the _____.
10. (Add 3 letters.) Do you believe that we will have six more weeks of winter if the _____ sees his shadow on February 2?

Related Words

g _____
g _____

Rhymes

g _____   d _____
h _____   _____
d _____   h _____
_____   _____
_____   _____

Many movies are made in Hollyw_____, California.
We won the basketball game because our star player got the reb_____.

Lesson 43

Name _____

| a | o | o | u | u | b | b | n | r | r | s | s | t |

Make Words

1. In a foot race, we see who can _____ the fastest.
2. (Change 1 letter.) We grilled the hot dog and put it in a _____.
3. (Add 1 letter.) If you have the heat too high, the hot dog might _____.
4. (Change 1 letter.) Go to the end of the street and make a right _____.
5. Plants have stems, leaves, and _____.
6. (Change 1 letter.) I put on my _____ to go out and play in the snow.
7. (Change 1 letter.) The Pilgrims crossed the ocean in small _____.
8. (Move the letters.) Another word for brag is _____.
9. (Change 1 letter.) My mom cooked a pot _____ for dinner.
10. One of the largest dinosaurs was named _____.

Rhymes

r _____

t _____

b _____

r _____

We put suntan lotion on because we don't want to get a sunb_____.
For breakfast, I had peanut butter and jelly on t_____.

Name _____

e	u	b	f	l	r	t	t	y

Make Words

1. In school, I always t_____ and do my best work.
2. (Change 1 letter.) We could bake the chicken or we could _____ it.
3. (Change 1 letter.) A fish can swim and a bird can _____.
4. The color purple is a combination of red and _____.
5. (Change the first 2 letters.) The opposite of false is _____.
6. When I get dressed up, I wear a _____ to hold up my pants.
7. (Change 1 letter.) I had a headache and a sore throat, and I _____ awful.
8. (Move the letters.) Go to the end of the street and make a _____ turn.
9. A t_____ is an animal that can pull its body inside its shell.
10. When a baby caterpillar is grown, it turns into a _____.

We found a good cl_____ which helped us solve the mystery.
When the temperatures get above freezing, the snow will m_____.

Related Words

f _____

f _____

Rhymes

t _____

_____

_____

b _____

b _____

_____

Name _____

e	e	e	e	n	n	s	t	y

Make Words

1. The number after nine is _____.
2. (Add 1 letter.) When I turn thirteen, I will be a _____.
3. (Change 1 letter.) Has anyone _____ _____ the new movie?
4. The policeman wore a bulletproof _____ _____.
5. (Change 1 letter.) The baby birds were all in their _____ _____.
6. (Move the letters.) I _____ _____ my grandma a birthday card.
7. One, three, and five are odd numbers, but two, four, and six are _____ _____ numbers.
8. (Add 1 letter.) The opening of the big, new mall was a great _____ _____ for our town.
9. Three plus four equals _____ _____ _____.
10. (Add 4 letters.) I will be _____ _____ _____ when I graduate from high school.

Related Words

s _____ _____ _____

t _____ _____

s _____ _____ _____ _____

s _____ _____ _____

Rhymes

v _____ _____

s _____ _____ _____

s _____ _____ _____

_____ _____ _____

We watched the game on a big scr_____ TV.
In science, we did a neat experim_____.

a	e	o	o	h	p	s	t	t	t

Make Words

1. The baby was wearing a _____ to protect her head from the sun.

2. (Change 1 letter.) I love to swim on a very _____ day.

3. (Change 1 letter.) We cooked the soup in a big _____.

4. To get to school, we walk p_____ a big park.

5. (Add 1 letter.) We used _____ to put our valentine hearts on our cards.

6. (Change 1 letter.) The milk was sour and did not _____ good.

7. (Move the letters.) Hawaii became a _____ in 1959.

8. I had to go to the dentist because my back right t_____ was really hurting me.

9. Today the temperature hit 102 degrees, and it was the _____ day we have had all summer.

10. Crest® and Colgate® are different kinds of _____.

Related Words

h _____

h _____

p _____

t _____

t _____ p _____

Rhymes

_____ h _____

_____ _____

p _____ _____

_____ _____

We had a water shortage and had to be careful not to w_____ water. I forg_____ to bring my lunch money.

Lesson 47

59

Name _____

a	a	e	c	c	k	r	r	t

Make Words

1. Every day after school, I take ———————————— of my little brother.

2. (Move the letters.) I ran fastest and won the ————————.

3. Squirrels use their sharp teeth to c ———————— nuts and eat them.

4. (Change 1 letter.) Every day during P. E., we run two laps around the ———————.

5. (Change 1 letter.) I can draw this horse if I ————————
over the picture from the book.

6. (Move the letters.) My bike came packed in a large ————————.

7. (Add 1 letter.) The volcano left a huge ————————
in the mountain.

8. I got a new tennis r ———————— for my birthday.

9. He is good at k ———————— and has already won a
black belt.

10. The cars were racing around the ————————.

Related Words

r ———— ————

t ———— ————

r ———— ———— t ————

Rhymes

r ———— ————

c

r ————

c

Lesson 48

I carry all my books in my backp————————.
The place where you are born is called your birthpl————————.

Name ————————

a	e	i	o	c	m	r	v	w

Make Words

1. In the summer, one of my jobs is to m _____ the grass.

2. (Change 1 letter.) Our seats are in the fourth _____.

3. (Add 1 letter.) A big, black _____ flew over the field.

4. My mother called and said it was time for me to _____ home.

5. (Change 1 letter.) The middle of the apple is called the _____.

6. (Change 1 letter.) Could I please have some _____ ice cream?

7. (Change 1 letter.) My friend is going to _____ to another state.

8. (Add 1 letter.) This Saturday, we are going to see a scary _____.

9. Be sure to put the c _____ on the pan to keep the food warm.

10. I made the popcorn in the _____ oven.

Rhymes

m _____

_____

_____

c _____

_____

_____

I have to walk the dog bef _____ I go to school every morning.
Sometimes after it rains, there is a bright rainb _____ in the sky.

Lesson 49

Name _____

© Carson-Dellosa CD-2611

61

a	e	e	i	o	f	g	r	r	r	t

Make Words

1. It was hard to see because the whole area was covered in _____.

2. (Add 1 letter.) The tadpole turned into a _ _ _ _.

3. The swing was under a big oak _ _ _ _.

4. (Change 1 letter.) It didn't cost anything because it was _ _ _ _.

5. It took the firefighters three days to put out the big _ _ _ _.

6. (Change 1 letter.) We were late because we had a flat _ _ _ _.

7. The mother t _ _ _ _ was taking care of her baby cubs.

8. The opposite of remember is f _ _ _ _ _.

9. A fox t _ _ _ _ _ is a very small dog.

10. We put things in the _ _ _ _ _ _ _ to keep them cold.

Rhymes

f _ _ _

_ _ _ _

f _ _ _

_ _ _ _

f _ _ _ _

We ordered the camping equipment from a catal_____.

It came and everything had a money-back guarant_____.

Lesson 50

Name _____

Warm-Up Lessons

1. **Made Words:** it, lit, hit, tin, thin, thing, night, light, lighting, lightning **Related Words:** light, lighting, lightning **Rhymes:** it, lit, hit; light, night; tin, thin **Transfer Words:** quit, fight

2. **Made Words:** some, sing, thin, hint, mint, might, sight, night, thing, something **Related Words:** some, thing, something **Rhymes:** mint, hint; sing, thing; night, might, sight **Transfer Words:** footprint, flashlight

3. **Made Words:** us, bus, sub, tub, tubs, stub, test, best, tube, substitute, **Rhymes:** us, bus; best, test; sub, tub, stub **Transfer Words:** club, west

4. **Made Words:** pin, spin, sore, rose, nose, pine, spine, siren, prison, prisoners **Related Words:** prison, prisoners **Rhymes:** pin, spin; pine, spine; rose, nose **Transfer Words:** sunshine, close

5. **Made Words:** hid, hide, side, wide, wise, dish, wash, wish, wishes, dishwasher **Related Words:** hid, hide; wish, wishes; dish, wash, dishwasher **Rhymes:** dish, wish; hide, side, wide **Transfer Words:** divide, jellyfish

Lessons

1. **Made Words:** ate, art, mart, smart, start, state, taste, matter, mattress, smartest **Related Words:** smart, smartest **Rhymes:** ate, state; art, mart, smart, start **Transfer Words:** gate, chart

2. **Made Words:** cat, act, ate, rate, cave, crave, crate, create, active, creative, **Related Words:** act, active; create, creative **Rhymes:** ate, rate, crate; cave, crave **Transfer Words:** decorate, behave

3. **Made Words:** eat, heat, heap, cheap, peach, reach, teach, Earth, chapter, parachute **Rhymes:** eat, heat; heap, cheap; peach, reach, teach **Transfer Words:** bleach, leap

4. **Made Words:** set, vet, eat, cat, scat, seat, save, cave, visit, cavities **Rhymes:** set, vet; cat, scat; eat, seat; save, cave **Transfer Words:** jet, flat, brave

5. **Made Words:** lap, lip, clip, clap, nail, pail, pain, plain, panic, principal **Rhymes:** lap, clap; lip, clip; nail, pail; pain, plain **Transfer Words:** trail, remain

6. **Made Words:** tie, sit, quit, note, nose, quiet, quite, quote, untie, questions **Related Words:** tie, untie **Rhymes:** sit, quit; note, quote **Transfer Words:** remote, admit

7. **Made Words:** red, rid, hid, hide, hive, dive, diver, drive, shiver, shivered **Related Words:** hid, hide; dive, diver; shiver, shivered **Rhymes:** rid, hid; hive, dive, drive **Transfer Words:** survive, pyramid

8. **Made Words:** pin, nip, rip, ripe, pipe, open, opener, pepper, pioneer, pepperoni **Related Words:** open, opener; pepper, pepperoni **Rhymes:** nip, rip; pipe, ripe **Transfer Words:** wipe, spaceship

9. **Made Words:** oil, soil, sail, rail, road, load, radio, radar, sailor, railroads **Related Words:** sail, sailor; rail, road, railroads **Rhymes:** oil, soil; rail, sail; road, load **Transfer Words:** jail, spoil

10. **Made Words:** at, ate, eat, heat, neat, late, hate, health, healthy, unhealthy **Related Words:** health, healthy, unhealthy **Rhymes:** ate, hate, late; eat, heat, neat **Transfer Words:** skate, treat

11. **Made Words:** test, rest, pest, step, steep, sheep, short, sport, mother, stepmother **Related Words:** mother, stepmother **Rhymes:** test, rest, pest; steep, sheep; short, sport **Transfer Words:** report, arrest

12. **Made Words:** bee, see, seen, sing, ring, bring, begin, green, engine, beginners **Related Words:** see, seen; begin, beginners **Rhymes:** bee, see; sing, ring, bring; seen, green **Transfer Words:** between, referee

13. **Made Words:** did, hid, hide, side, wide, wind, slide, hidden, inside, windshield **Related Words:** hid, hide, hidden; wind, windshield **Rhymes:** did, hid; hide, side, wide, slide, inside **Transfer Words:** divide, eyelid

14. **Made Words:** lie, tie, time, lime, mile, miles, smile, slime, motel, mistletoe **Rhymes:** lie, tie; time, lime, slime; mile, smile **Transfer Words:** crocodile, reptile

15. **Made Words:** go, ago, zoo, zip, lip, log, leg, age, page, apologize **Rhymes:** zip, lip; age, page **Transfer Words:** trip, stage

16. **Made Words:** end, send, note, nose, hose, shoe, dish, dishes, honest, dishonest **Related Words:** dish, dishes; honest, dishonest **Rhymes:** end, send; nose, hose **Transfer Words:** chose, pretend

17. **Made Words:** do, cry, dry, dive, drive, cried, dries, cover, discover, discovery **Related Words:** dry, dries; cry, cried; cover, discover, discovery **Rhymes:** cry, dry; dive, drive **Transfer Words:** pry, arrive

18. **Made Words:** go, goes, gone, sore, rose, nose, noose, goose, govern, governors **Related Words:** go, goes, gone; govern, governors **Rhymes:** nose, rose; noose, goose **Transfer Words:** loose, hose

19. **Made Words:** sore, rose, lose, wore, weep, sweep, sleep, power, losers, powerless **Related Words:** lose, losers; power, powerless **Rhymes:** sore, wore; weep, sweep, sleep **Transfer Words:** jeep, store

20. **Made Words:** all, age, cage, call, hall, eagle, angle, angel, change, challenge **Rhymes:** all, call, hall; age, cage **Transfer Words:** football, stage

21. **Made Words:** ice, mice, rice, race, lace, lame, meal, real, Memorial, commercial **Rhymes:** ice, mice, rice; meal, real; race, lace **Transfer Words:** appeal, birthplace

22. **Made Words:** sad, rag, drag, grad, read, dear, grade, agree, agreed, disagree **Related Words:** agree, agreed, disagree **Rhymes:** sad, grad; rag, drag **Transfer Words:** brag, granddad

23. **Made Words:** hit, rest, best, sight, right, tiger, hitter, bitter, bright, brightest **Related Words:** hit, hitter; bright, brightest **Rhymes:** best, rest; right, sight, bright; hitter, bitter **Transfer Words:** babysitter, contest

63

24. **Made Words:** song, sing, ring, hero, born, horn, horse, bones, singer, neighbors **Related Words:** song, sing, singer **Rhymes:** sing, ring; born, horn **Transfer Words:** popcorn, anything

25. **Made Words:** it, lit, pit, pool, tool, upon, until, pilot, lotion, pollution **Rhymes:** it, lit, pit; pool, tool **Transfer Words:** admit, school

26. **Made Words:** dip, hip, ship, here, hire, wire, wish, wished, whisper, whispered **Related Words:** wish, wished; whisper, whispered **Rhymes:** hire, wire; dip, hip, ship **Transfer Words:** retire, trip

27. **Made Words:** fan, can, cat, fat, fast, cats, cast, acts, facts, fantastic **Related Words:** fan, fantastic **Rhymes:** fan, can; acts, facts; fast, cast; cat, fat **Transfer Words:** past, Batman, Superman

28. **Made Words:** go, goes, ears, gears, sound, round, around, ground, danger, dangerous **Related Words:** go, goes; danger, dangerous **Rhymes:** ears, gears; sound, round, around, ground **Transfer Words:** rebound, disappears

29. **Made Words:** far, fear, near, nest, rest, star, stare, after, faster, transfer **Rhymes:** far, star; fear, near; nest, rest **Transfer Words:** year, car, west

30. **Made Words:** ear, hear, heal, real, seal, leash, share, erase, eraser, rehearsal **Related Words:** erase, eraser **Rhymes:** ear, hear; real, seal, heal **Transfer Words:** oatmeal, disappear

31. **Made Words:** eat, tie, sit, site, neat, quit, quite, quiet, untie, antiques **Related Words:** tie, untie **Rhymes:** eat, neat; sit, quit; site, quite **Transfer Words:** satellite, mistreat

32. **Made Words:** eat, seat, neat, ants, tent, rent, eaten, neater, neatest, anteaters **Related Words:** ants, anteaters; eat, eaten, anteaters; neat, neater, neatest **Rhymes:** eat, seat, neat; rent, tent **Transfer Words:** experiment, invent

33. **Made Words:** bill, bull, full, fill, fight, night, light, flight, fighting, bullfighting **Related Words:** fight, fighting, bullfighting; bull, bullfighting **Rhymes:** bull, full; bill, fill; night, fight, light, flight **Transfer Words:** thrill, pull

34. **Made Words:** old, bold, sell, bell, bull, loud, older, louder, double, bulldozers **Related Words:** old, older; loud, louder; bull, bulldozers **Rhymes:** bell, sell; old, bold **Transfer Words:** blindfold, cell

35. **Made Words:** ate, late, tale, tail, nail, alien, dance, cancel, accident, accidental **Related Words:** accident, accidental **Rhymes:** ate, late; nail, tail **Transfer Words:** monorail, translate

36. **Made Words:** car, cat, rat, art, cart, star, start, strict, artist, artistic **Related Words:** art, artist, artistic **Rhymes:** cat, rat; car, star; art, cart, start **Transfer Words:** superstar, habitat

37. **Made Words:** ate, Abe, able, late, plate, table, cable, palace, accept, acceptable **Related Words:** accept, acceptable **Rhymes:** ate, late, plate; able, table, cable **Transfer Words:** stable, migrate

38. **Made Words:** yes, you, nuts, guts, gets, nets, nest, guest, young, youngest **Related Words:** young, youngest **Rhymes:** nuts, guts; gets, nets; nest, guest **Transfer Words:** haircuts, arrest

39. **Made Words:** tire, fire, tree, free, flee, feel, feet, fleet, retire, fertilizer **Rhymes:** free, tree, flee; feet, fleet; tire, fire, retire **Transfer Words:** parakeet, umpire

40. **Made Words:** bug, hug, huge, rush, brush, cheers, rescue, secure, cheese, cheeseburger **Related Words:** cheese, cheeseburger **Rhymes:** bug, hug; rush, brush **Transfer Words:** unplug, flush

41. **Made Words:** rat, art, part, trap, strap, parts, sport, short, graphs, photographs **Related Words:** graphs, photographs **Rhymes:** art, part; trap, strap; sport, short **Transfer Words:** kidnap, passport

42. **Made Words:** all, mall, small, rules, mules, album, lumber, rumble, smaller, umbrellas **Related Words:** small, smaller **Rhymes:** all, mall, small; rules, mules **Transfer Words:** basketball, baseball, football

43. **Made Words:** dog, hog, hug, dug, good, hood, hound, round, ground, groundhog **Related Words:** ground, groundhog **Rhymes:** good, hood; dug, hug; dog, hog; hound, round, ground **Transfer Words:** Hollywood, rebound

44. **Made Words:** run, bun, burn, turn, roots, boots, boats, boast, roast, brontosaurus **Rhymes:** run, bun; turn, burn; boots, roots; roast, boast **Transfer Words:** sunburn, toast

45. **Made Words:** try, fry, fly, blue, true, belt, felt, left, turtle, butterfly **Related Words:** fly, butterfly **Rhymes:** try, fry, fly; blue, true; belt, felt **Transfer Words:** clue, melt

46. **Made Words:** ten, teen, seen, vest, nest, sent, even, event, seven, seventeen **Related Words:** seven, teen, seventeen **Rhymes:** vest, nest; sent, event; seen, teen, seventeen **Transfer Words:** screen, experiment

47. **Made Words:** hat, hot, pot, past, paste, taste, state, tooth, hottest, toothpaste **Related Words:** hot, hottest; paste, tooth, toothpaste **Rhymes:** hot, pot; paste, taste **Transfer Words:** waste, forgot

48. **Made Words:** care, race, crack, track, trace, crate, crater, racket, karate, racetrack **Related Words:** race, track, racetrack **Rhymes:** race, trace; crack, track, racetrack **Transfer Words:** backpack, birthplace

49. **Made Words:** mow, row, crow, come, core, more, move, movie, cover, microwave **Rhymes:** mow, row, crow; core, more **Transfer Words:** before, rainbow

50. **Made Words:** fog, frog, tree, free, fire, tire, tiger, forget, terrier, refrigerator **Rhymes:** free, tree; fire, tire; fog, frog **Transfer Words:** catalog, guarantee